MY FULL NAME IS:

Abigail Jane Delizio

MY NAME MEANS:

my father's joy

MY BIRTH DATE IS:

09 / 29 / 1997

**Not one person is an accident.
No matter what circumstances you were born
into, you have a purpose, a plan from God, and a
wonderful destiny.**

For my four beautiful children…
Charles, Grace, River & Faith.

Because the wonder of YOU takes my breath away.

Because the privilege of being your mom leaves me grateful.

Because the endless possibilities of God partnering with you keep me dreaming and praying.

Because our family has a legacy to continue a vibrant faith-walk with Christ until He returns to Earth.

That God let me be your Mom blows me away, because we all know just how imperfect I am.

May you always know how incredible and loved you are.

I hope you dig up and discover all the treasures God placed inside of you. Love you more…

Mom

This is no ordinary book.

This book is for you. It's all about you.

It's something for you to write in, get messy, and put down your thoughts. You have permission to "dog-ear the pages," doodle in the margins, cross out your answers, and write again.

That's because you are going to go on a journey. And I'm not talking about taking a vacation. You're going to explore YOU. You're going to find out what makes you special. And like investigating the inside of a watch or robot, we are going to check out the inside of YOU - how God wired you to hum, tick & flow just right.

In these pages, you will discover the answers to questions like…

What are the gifts hidden inside of me?
Why did the Creator make me this way?
What is God's plan for my life?
How do I recognize His voice?
How can I get God's help in tough situations?
What do I do with all the dreams I have for the future?

By the time you are finished with this process, the book you hold in your hands will be a KEEPSAKE - a memoir of this amazing season in your life.

Welcome to the journey called "YOUnique."

ITEMS EVERY YOUNG ADULT WILL NEED FOR EACH SMALL GROUP SESSION:

Pencil or Pen
Mobile device that can connect to the internet
(computer, ipod, smart-phone, tablet, etc)
This book

HOW TO GET THE MOST OUT OF THIS BOOK...

Go through this experience with friends! This book is written as a "small-group experience" where two or more young adults can get together in a home or casual setting with little distraction. Provide some snacks if you can, since everyone loves a little food. Pick a day and time you can commit to meeting for 8 weeks straight. The total time needed each week is about an hour and a half - fifteen minutes for socializing and snacks, one hour maximum for the study, and fifteen minutes at the end for fun!

Commit to attending all 8 weeks. The teaching builds on itself and you don't want to miss one element of FUN! *(If you must miss, the video teaching is available on-line to watch at a separate time.)*

An adult is encouraged to facilitate the gathering, as there is some interaction needed, and guidance will be necessary while students are using mobile devices to take various personality and gift tests. The Small Group Leader will also need access to a computer or larger screen to show the weekly video session to the group.

Parents or guardians are strongly urged to watch their own video introduction found on our website. It will help them understand what the YOUnique experience is all about, and provide important tips in order for the students to get the most out of this incredible program.

Coordinating videos and extra content are available on our website at www.YOUniquelyDesigned.org

CHAPTERS

"BEFORE I SHAPED YOU IN THE WOMB, I KNEW ALL ABOUT YOU. BEFORE YOU SAW THE LIGHT OF DAY, I HAD HOLY PLANS FOR YOU."

JEREMIAH 1:5 (MSG)

CHAPTER 1

YOUR PERSONALITY

Group Reading
(If you are in a group study, this section is for you all to read together - out loud. Go around the room and each of you read a paragraph at a time. Take your time so everyone can hear and understand. Let's get this party started!)

You…You didn't just show up on this planet. There's a reason you are here. While your mom and dad played the role of helping you get here, **you were conceived in the heart of God long before you were conceived on the earth.**

CHECK OUT THIS SCRIPTURE…

"Your eyes saw my unformed body; all the days ordained for me were written in your book before one of them came to be."
Psalm 139:16 (NIV)

Before you ever lived a moment with breath, God had a book written with your name in it. The days of your life were counted and measured. He chose you with special plans in mind that ONLY YOU can fulfill…for this time..for a purpose. This book contains the details of each day and all the good things He has planned for every moment of your life. Each day has significance. Each day has value. Each day is important.

> **"A person's days are determined;**
> **You have decreed the number of his**
> **months and have set limits**
> **he cannot exceed."**
> Job 14:5 (NIV)

God's plan is so intricate that for every person that has ever lived or will live, He has determined their time in history and their place in the events of the world. Yet with so many people who have lived and will ever live on earth - each is like no other. Each plan is so individual, so personal.

That's why there is no substitute for YOU. You are one of a kind. You are unique. For this book, I'm gonna call you YOUnique because I really hope to get into your head how special YOU are — not someone else. I'm talking right to you.

If you haven't already filled out the page with your name on it, go back a few pages and do it now. Take a few minutes to Google the meaning of your names and fill those in, too. Then continue…

Group Reading
You've probably studied a lot of different subjects in school. But have you studied YOU? Think about it. We spend years in elementary school, middle school, high school, and then college preparing for careers and a future. But how well do you know

yourself? Do you know what motivates you? Do you know why you get along with certain types of people, and not others? Do you know what helps you feel loved? Do you know what gifts you have been given by your Creator? Do you know how to hear the whispers your Creator sends to you to help you on your path? Do you know how to make the best impact on this earth with what God already put inside your skin?

Over the next 8 weeks, we are going to answer these questions, and start you on a really fun adventure! You will probably be surprised to discover things about yourself, and also be reminded of qualities you have, but perhaps never articulated. One of the fun elements in this adventure is that you are going to write all these discoveries down in one place - this book! You will be able to hold in your hands a "YOUnique" blue-print of your life.

Since we are trying to find out about YOU, it is important to understand that who you are has little to do with what your friends think about you, what your parents or teachers may say, or what your life looks like right now.

If you are lucky, you may have friends or family that say nice things about you. They may compliment you or point out your good qualities. But some of you are not so lucky. We've all had people put us down, whether they mean to or not. I encourage you to put out of your mind any negative thoughts you've had about yourself, and dismiss any words spoken to you that put down your abilities or physical appearance.

To find out about who you are, you have to go straight to the source of your life - the Creator Himself. The circumstances and people around you can help make you into something, but only if you LET them. We need to first hear what is true so that everything else we see or hear can be compared to that. Think of it this way: If an architect made a blueprint for a tall building, someone could look at the design and make fun of it. "What a terrible bridge!" they might say. But that's because they don't know that the architect designed it to be a building, not a bridge!

You have to find out about your own design and not let yourself or anyone else make comparisons. Comparing a building to a bridge would be silly, wouldn't it? Well, it's the same with you.

Let's start to look at YOUR design and let the architect who wrote out YOUR plan help you see what He designed you to be.

Take a pencil or pen and draw over your entire thumb. Press your thumb print right here.

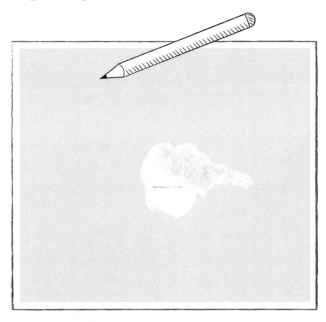

Small Group Leader, go to the "Small Group Leader" tab on our website and click on Chapter 1, Video Link #1.

VIDEO SESSION NOTES

I am _____ - _____ - ____ - _____

God does not make duplicates!

I am a _____ - _____ being

I am a _____

I have a _____

I live in a _____

We are made for _____

My soul contains my _____,
_____, and _____.

What is the question t   myself?

_____   _____

_____

_____

Group Reading

Now that the video session is over… Each of you take out a computer or mobile device. It's time to have some fun and begin the discovery!

Go to our website and click on the "Students Only" tab. Find the "Web Links Section" and click on Link #3 under Chapter 1. Read out loud the section that says, "What is your Teen's Personality Type?" It is a great way to understand the different types of personalities before you begin. Read until you reach "16 Different Personality Types."

Now, it's time to take the Personality Test. Remember, there are no right or wrong answers. Click on Link #2 under Chapter 1 and answer the questions. When you are finished, fill out your personality assessment results here. Have fun!

MY PERSONALITY PROFILE IS:

_____

THAT MEANS I:

_____

_____

_____

Group Reading
Before you leave tonight, split up into groups of two or three.
Share your personality profile with one another and share one
discovery you made about yourself.

THERE IS NO SUBSTITUTE FOR YOU. YOU ARE ONE—OF—A—KIND, BORN ON PURPOSE FOR A PURPOSE.

When you go home..
Tell your parents which personality type you are!

CHAPTER 2

YOUR LOVE LANGUAGE

Group Reading

Welcome back! Last week, we discovered your personality type. This week, we're going to learn about your personal "Love Language." Before you get creeped out at those words, let's talk a bit about your relationships - **the people you know and spend time with.**

Relationships are the key to everything that makes your life happy. How you relate to your parents, your siblings, your friends, teachers and strangers is preparing you for how you will relate to others the rest of your life. This may not seem important now, but trust me, it is!

You can make all the money in the world, and be the most popular person on the planet, but if you don't know how to treat people, or receive love from them, you will soon find yourself lonely and unhappy. The best things in life are meant to be enjoyed with other people. It's how God designed us. It's part of His YOUnique plan.

The second commandment in the Bible is to "love your neighbor as you love yourself." For this week, we will discuss the part about loving others. In our Week 4 study, we are going to discuss how to love ourselves.

A publication of the American Health Association says that "Relationships are - not surprisingly - enormously important for health…." The writer also goes on to say that the quality of our personal relationships also has an enormous impact on our physical health. So, science proves that even our bodies flourish best when we have healthy friendships and relationships. **Loving others and receiving love are crucial to your well-being.**

The word "love" probably brings up different ideas in each of your minds. For some, it may bring images of romance, for others thoughts of your faithful dog, or it may make you think of sweet friendships. For this chapter, we are going to define love as "the need that all of us have to be valued, feel connected to others, and be accepted without any motive or hidden agenda." That is a base need we all have - yes, even the toughest, roughest guy in the room. (You know who you are!)

When Jesus came to earth, there were a few things He stressed to the people around Him.

One was this…

> **"A new commandment I give to you, that you love one another."**
> John 13:34-35 (ESV)

Maybe this was a new thought for people at that time. Were they so busy trying to do all the right things for God that perhaps they didn't know how to show love to the person next to them? Why would it take being TOLD to love someone if it came naturally? And if you're like me, you might be asking yourself, "How do I love someone? What does it look like?"

Try to put yourself in the shoes of one of two brothers as you consider this scenario: It's the end of summer, and your older sibling is going off to college. Despite the fact that you have your arguments, deep down, you know you love him. You want to show him that he's actually going to be missed so you decide to wash his car and detail it. It takes you a long time. But it's worth it to you. As you scrub it down, and vacuum the interior, you remember some great memories together. **You think he's going to be so happy.** In the meantime, he walks up to you and hardly notices the sweat dripping from your face. "What are you doing in my car?" he asks. You explain the hard work you are doing for him, **but he doesn't seem to appreciate it the way you thought.** In the meantime, he hands you a note and slaps you on the back. "I'm sure gonna miss you. I wrote down some things that I think make you special so you don't forget."

"Gee, thanks," you tell yourself sarcastically. You don't say much to him as he drives off in his sparkling clean vehicle, but you get the feeling that neither of you quite appreciated each other's gifts like they were intended.

What went wrong? Clearly both of you were thinking of the other person. **The problem is that you were each speaking a language that the other was not able to hear.** How frustrating!

To avoid a life-time of scenarios happening like this,

we are going to go on a journey that just might blow your mind. Get ready to watch the video lesson for today. Don't forget to keep your books open and take notes.

Small Group Leader, go to the "Small Group Leader" tab on our website and click on Chapter 2, Video Link #1.

VIDEO SESSION NOTES:

Love has a _____

We all receive love _____

Since God gave us the responsibility to love ourselves and others, then it's our job to find out:

1. What makes _____ feel loved.
2. What makes _____ feel loved.

According to Gary Chapman, there are _____ basic love languages. They are:
1. _____
2. _____
3. _____
4. _____
5. _____

Best of all, once you've learned what your love language is, you can

_____ _____ _____

what works for you!

Group Reading

Go to our website and click on the "Students Only" tab. Find the "Web Links" section and click on Link #2. To get the most accurate results, answer the questions imagining your PARENTS or GUARDIANS doing those things for you. If you are not one of the ages listed, choose the age you are closest to being. When you are finished, your score will be on the top left of the screen. Fill out your discovery here:

MY TOP 2 LOVE LANGUAGES:

_____

_____

Group Reading:

Before you leave tonight, split up in groups of two or three. Share your love language with one another, and share one discovery you made about yourself. **Were you surprised at your answer?**

EXTRAS:

Go to the "Extras" tab on our website to watch some fun, animated, short videos that describe what YOUR love language is!

THE BEST THINGS IN LIFE ARE MEANT TO BE ENJOYED WITH OTHER PEOPLE.

CHAPTER 3

AGE LIMITATIONS & YOUR SPIRITUAL GIFTS

Group Reading

Hi again! I have a love/hate relationship with puzzles. I hate the part when you dump all the pieces out of the box and have to turn them over to see the picture side. I hate having to sort them into "border pieces" or "inside pieces." I hate having to sort them into matching colors. But then it happens…I spot two pieces that fit together, and BOOM! I'm hooked. I get all excited and start pouring over the pieces to find the next piece that fits in with the others. Somehow this painful experience turns into a fun game, and I am drawn back to those puzzle pieces until every last one is put together. Voila! The picture is complete.

Let's imagine now that the world is a big puzzle, and the people on earth (all seven and a half billion of them) are the pieces. **God's perfect plan is for each of us to be an individually, colorful piece that fits perfectly with other pieces around us.** Have you ever thought how much better the world would be if we all knew our own purpose and lived it out? God made us in this world to work together, and if you are the best **you** and I'm the best **me**, our world would be its best. The colorful pieces would interact perfectly to create a picture that is beautiful and crystal clear.

Everyone has a gift that someone else needs. Did you hear that? Maybe you thought you didn't have any gifts. Maybe you thought your gifts were only for yourself. God made us to feel most happy doing what we're good at. But, actually the greatest happiness is when we use our gifts to help others. (Imagine again when one puzzle piece attaches to another. It helps the big picture make sense!)

You are YOUniquely designed to use your specific gifts to impact the people and world around you for good.

CHECK OUT THIS SCRIPTURE...

"Each of you should use whatever gift you have received to serve others, as faithful stewards of God's grace in its various forms"

1 Peter 4:10 (NIV)

Hans Urs von Balthasar said a famous quote: "What you are is God's gift to you; what you become is your gift to God."

Did you ever think that one of God's best gifts to you was your life? And to develop it and use it for others is YOUR GIFT TO HIM?

Wow. That's amazing. Right now, you are filled with potential, and you get to choose to partner with your Creator and use all that's in you for His glory. That's why we're in this discovery process called Younique!

Let's start with this whole age thing. Some of you may be tempted to think, "This stuff is all good and well, but I'm too young. How can I really help people around me? How can I really impact the WORLD at this age? This is for later on in my life, right?" Wrong. I want to seriously crush the thought that you are too young to make a difference right now. I want to crush it to the ground and pound it until it's fine powder and blows away forever. Yes, that's aggressive, I know. :)

If you believe the lie that you can only be used by God LATER in life, you can develop the attitude that puts off your value TODAY. And today is all you have. Tomorrow isn't here yet.

There is no place in the Bible saying that God only uses people at a certain age. **There is no age limit for purpose or calling.** In other words, God doesn't say you're too young for Him to use you. Actually, we find the opposite in the Bible. Let's look at a few examples...

"You have taught children and infants to tell of your strength, silencing your enemies and all who oppose you."
Psalm 8:2 (NLT)

This verse says that even infants have a capacity to do a powerful work for God. Say what???

"And the child Samuel ministered unto the Lord before Eli. And the word of the Lord was precious in those days; there was no open vision...Now the Lord came and stood and called as at other times,
"Samuel! Samuel!" And Samuel answered,
"Speak, for Your servant hears"
I Samuel 3:1, 10 (KJV & NKJV)

This is one of my favorite stories in the Bible. Samuel was a **boy** who learned to hear God's voice. People all over the world at that time were not hearing God's voice. He developed that skill as a child and was used as God's instrument to speak for Him his entire life long. But at first, he didn't even know who was talking to him!

In another example, a young servant girl told her master about God's healing power and helped him receive a radical healing in his body (II Kings 5).

At the age of 12, Jesus was in the temple talking to leaders who were wise and understood the Bible. They were amazed at his wisdom and insight. **The signs of His future were already being played out before he was even a teenager!** (Luke 2:41-52)

This next verse is for you to all read out loud. I encourage you to memorize it, think about it, and make it something you go back to again and again. Paul was telling this to a younger man he mentored. Here we go…

CHECK OUT THIS SCRIPTURE…

"Do not let anyone look down on you because you are young, but be an example for other believers in your speech, behavior, love, faithfulness, and purity."

1 Timothy 4:12 (ISV)

Go ahead and read that out loud again.

Does that mean you are hot stuff and should demand that everyone listen to you? No. It means that in humility, you must be confident that **you matter.** And you shouldn't let anyone mess with your mind to tell you that you are less important because of your age. Here is what is true.

You have a voice - something worthwhile to say.

There's a place for you - a part in this world that needs you and you alone.

God wants to fill you and use you TODAY.

Life TODAY is better because you are around!

You have something YOUnique to give to others that no one else can give.

Don't let others say what you can't do based on their ideas of age limitation. God can use **anyone** who humbly walks with Him and asks Him for His help.

Now that we've established that your age has nothing to do with God's ability to use you, let's go on to this concept of gifting. Let's watch today's video teaching.

Small Group Leader, go to the "Small Group Leader" tab on our website and click on Chapter 3, Video Link #1.

You may need to pause the video while the students are filling in the blanks.

VIDEO SESSION NOTES:

The spiritual gifts God has given people include:

_____ to steer, rule or direct others towards a goal; similar to leadership, but it is more concerned with details of HOW to get where you're going

_____ understanding

_____ plants new ministries; leader of leaders; able to take risk and perform difficult tasks; entrepreneur

_____ people-oriented; leads others well; visionary

_____ able to discern or appraise a person or situation; might notice things others don't

_____ patient and compassionate to others who are suffering; concern for physical and spiritual needs of others

_____ able to overcome normal fear of rejection to talk to others about God

_____ to encourage, lift up or motivate others

_____ similar to leadership and teaching; keeps a look out for others; cares for the hurting, guides people to new healthy places in their life

_____ has special confidence and trust in God to see Him go above and beyond the ordinary; believes easily in the miraculous and helps others do the same

_____ generous without any pretense; loves to share with others and has a pure motive doing it

_____ naturally enjoys doing acts of service to help community; enjoys helping out others; can be content to serve in the background especially if they see how they're contributing to the big picture

_____ effectively communicates, explains, instructs, and speaks to others' hearts

_____ to speak to someone's life with the goal of helping guide them toward good

Group Reading

It's time for you to discover your YOUnique spiritual gifts!
Go to our website and click on the "Students Only" tab. Find the "Web Links" section and click on Link #3. When the site opens, click the button that says "Register as a guest."

MY TOP SPIRITUAL GIFTS ARE:

_____

_____

_____

_____

_____

How can you use your gift this week to help others?

_____

_____

Group Reading

As you close up tonight, get together in groups of 2 or 3 and tell one another what your top spiritual gifts are. Were you surprised by the results of your test? Share your answer to the question above and help each other come up with ways to use your gift this week.

LIFE TODAY
IS BETTER
BECAUSE
YOU
ARE IN IT.

CHAPTER 4

ACCEPTING YOUR YOUNIQUENESS

Small Group Leader, for this lesson, you are going to need the ability to play worship music. Please pick quieter, reflective songs that kids are currently singing in their worship experience at church, or choose from one of the YouTube links provided on our web-site under the "Small Group Leader" tab. There are some times of reflection and prayer in this session, and a worshipful atmosphere can help prepare hearts to hear the Holy Spirit more easily. Thank you!

Group Reading
Welcome back! By now, you've had three weeks to discover things about yourself. Take a few minutes to go around the room and share one thing you found out that you didn't know before, or share one gift you have that became clear these last three weeks.

It's amazing how different we all are. We can look around a room and see the obvious differences in our hair, eyes, height and physical features, but by now I hope you're starting to look and see people in a whole new way. I hope you're beginning to see them for the incredible qualities they have on the inside. It can almost becomes a game. Ask yourself…

"What's hidden inside this person that is in front of me right now?"

You may be able to help **them** discover their YOUnique

qualities now that you are beginning to see your own.

It's kinda strange, though, that whether we are very confident with how we are made, or are still uncertain about ourselves, we ALL have a tendency to compare ourselves with others. Sometimes, we even wish we could be someone else. For example, you may have the gift of mercy. Perhaps you are more quiet and reserved, but you have a deep compassion for people. This compassion draws you to notice others, and helps you to enjoy deep friendships. **You easily move in this gift, and are confident doing so.**

But, then, you may see a person walk in a room and light it up as they speak confidently to everyone they encounter. Like a magnet, people are drawn to them, and suddenly, you lose your confidence. You feel less important. You feel inferior. You look at them and think, "I could NEVER do that. I wish I was like them."

In just a few seconds, you devalued yourself by looking at someone else's value and comparing yourself to them. Doing that is like comparing a strawberry and a piece of cheese, and saying that one is better than the other because they aren't the same. Some people would say the strawberry is much better because it is sweet and fresh. Others would argue that the cheese is better by far because it took time to age and the protein is better for the body. The truth is, they were never meant to be alike! They were both meant to be eaten (nom nom) but that's about the only similarity. They have different looks, different functions, different tastes, but are equally great food to be enjoyed!

This brings us to something EVERY one of us has to settle. Today, I pray that you have an open heart to hear this because it can help you avoid such heart-ache. Some of you are depressed or feel inadequate because of this one issue.

People spend years trying to impress others, act like others, and be what they are not…simply because they feel they are not adequate **JUST AS THEY ARE.** You could probably fill in the blanks.

I'm too _____. I'll never be _____. I'm not able to _____.

Could you put something in each of those sentences?

Let's start by reminding ourselves again that your existence here on earth was not by YOUR choice. God created the universe. He created you. And He created you for HIS purpose. If you ever wish you were made differently, this is an awesome Bible verse to know.

CHECK OUT THIS SCRIPTURE...

"For you created my inmost being; you knit me together in my mother's womb. I praise you because I am fearfully and wonderfully made; your works are wonderful, I know that full well."

Psalm 139:13-14 (NIV)

God intricately created each of you - every facet and detail. He wants you to know that you are made FEARFULLY. That word "fear" means awe-some…full of awe. Have you ever looked at a tiny baby's hands and thought, "How perfect are these little fingers?" It fills us with awe that something so delicate was created inside a mother. You were made in the most awe-some way. **God also wants you to know that you are made WONDERFULLY.** That word "wonderful' means set apart, distinguished, and a wondrous show. God showed off when He made you! He said "Check out this one. I set them apart from every other being. I am making a one-of-a-kind individual." Wouldn't it be sad to say to your Creator, "You did a bad job! This needs to be changed."

"How horrible it will be for the one who quarrels with his Maker. He is pottery among other earthenware pots. Does the clay ask the one who shapes it, "What are you making?"
Isaiah 45:9 (God's Word translation)

This is my interpretation of that verse: "Who are we to say to God, 'Why did you make me like this?' when **He has a specific plan for you being just the way you are."**

"But who are you, a human being, to talk back to God? "Shall what is formed say to the one who formed it,
'Why did you make me like this?'"
Rom. 9:20 (NIV)

When I was a teenager, I was horribly aware of my fair skin. Now, I don't have just fair skin. I have the kind of skin that GLOWS WHITE on the beach. If I sit on the white sand, my legs will disappear altogether because I'm so pale. That kind of skin did not do well for me in high school because the cool thing was to be TAN! Oh, how I wished to be tan and gorgeous! Instead, I was white and freckly. But then, I discovered something in the cosmetic aisle at the store one day. It was a "fake tanning cream." Now, if you're imagining the tanning lotions we have now in the stores, you are mistaken. This was the only tanning cream available that I knew of, and it made you ORANGE. I do mean orange. I was so thrilled to use it, though. ANY color was better than milk white - even orange! I was so proud of my new look. The only problem was that it washed off very easily and it stained my hands with a deep, dark (um) orange color. When I ran on the track team and started to perspire… you guessed it. The perspiration beads would create little white streaks on my legs. I was not tan anymore. I was striped! If I went to the beach, I would show up very orange (or "dark" as I put it). But by the end of the day, I would leave pale with a few orange smears to remind me that I once had tanning lotion on. It was pitiful. And it was agonizing because I was so aware of my skin that I couldn't enjoy the beach!

It wasn't until I really understood the love God had for me, and His full acceptance of me JUST AS I WAS, that I was healed in my heart.

When I received and understood My Creator's love, I went to the beach for the first time FREE! I remember wanting to play in the ocean, do cart wheels in the sand, and enjoy every moment - even though I still glowed white like a light bulb. My skin color no longer took my joy away. The disappointment in my looks could not steal my joy. I was less concerned about what other people thought of me because I was happy with what God thought of me. I was not bound by what anyone else thought, and I felt fully accepted and pleasing. That was all that mattered. It was the start of so many good changes inside me. THIS is God's heart for you, too. I know He wants you to be FREE, happy with yourself - just as you are right now.

Here's what He says to you...

> *"I have loved you with an ever lasting love;*
> *I have drawn you with unfailing kindness."*
> *Jeremiah 31:30 (NIV)*

His love for you began before time, and will exist for eternity. When you really understand that, you find freedom.

I want YOU to experience the same freedom I did. Have you thought that maybe God didn't do a good enough job when He created you? What do you find unpleasing about yourself?

Do you know God loves you completely without ever changing a thing? There's nothing you can do right now to make Him love you more or less.

Think about that, and while you do, you're going to watch a video. You are going to see the story of Nick Vujicic - a man born without arms and legs. See how he came to peace with how he was made, and watch how he has used his greatest challenge to be the catalyst for becoming a great speaker and business-man who influences people around the world. (Side note: Nick's turning point was when He encountered God and received His love, too!)

Small Group Leader, go to the "Small Group Leader" tab on our website and click on Chapter 4, then Video Link #1. When finished, watch Video Link #2.

After this video, encourage the students to quietly separate on their own to complete the next two pages. Be sure they each have a pen or pencil. Please turn on some quiet worship music for the sake of privacy and let them write in the next section on their own.

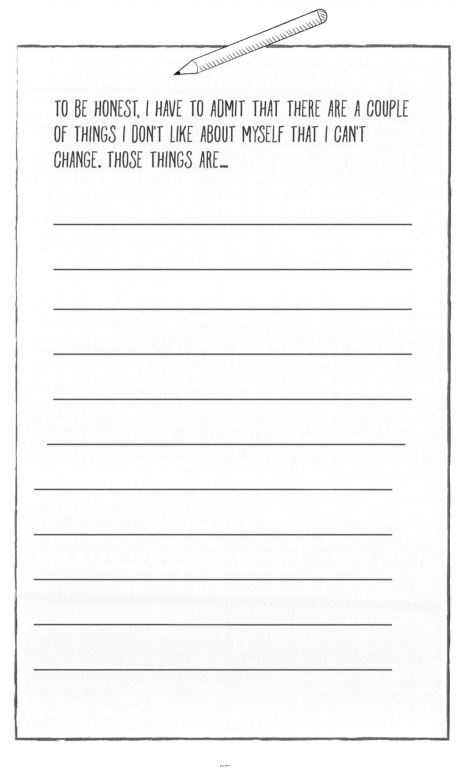

TO BE HONEST, I HAVE TO ADMIT THAT THERE ARE A COUPLE OF THINGS I DON'T LIKE ABOUT MYSELF THAT I CAN'T CHANGE. THOSE THINGS ARE...

PRAYER

"God, thank you for making me. Thank you for loving me just as I am. I have trouble accepting myself that way. There are parts about myself that I wish were made differently. Would you please help me. I find myself wanting to be more like others. Today, I want that to stop. I'm sorry that I looked at your creation (me) and said it wasn't good enough. Please forgive me. These are the things I haven't liked about myself....(Name the things you listed previously on the other page.) Since you are God and you know what's best for me, I am going to accept myself just as I am. I need your help with that. Please show me how I can use everything you gave me to help others and to please You. Help me to see the awe-someness You created when you made me. Help me to see that I am made wonderfully. Thank you for loving me.
In Jesus' name.
Amen.

Small Group Leader, after students finish this portion of the lession, gather them together before they leave. Ask them to write the answers to the questions on the following page. Encourage them to tell one person they trust THIS WEEK what they write down. Have a great week!`

WHAT HAS GOD DONE IN MY HEART TODAY?
WHAT AREA OF MY LIFE HAVE I COME TO PEACE WITH?

_____

_____

_____

_____

_____

_____

GOD CAREFULLY DESIGNED YOU — BODY, SOUL, AND SPIRIT TO BE A MASTERPIECE FOR HIM.

EXTRAS:

Some of you may want to dig deeper into the story of Nick Fujicic. He has some very inspiring videos that may help you as you walk out the issue of accepting how God made you. Go to our website, and click on the "Extras" tab to find the links...

CHAPTER 5
THE BEST GIFT

Group Reading

Imagine that it's your birthday. For months, you've been looking at something that you REALLY want. But it's very expensive, and you know there's no way you could actually afford it. You've hinted a little to others about it, but realized very quickly that it was not possible that someone could buy such an extravagant gift for you. You settle into a smug, "I don't care" attitude so that you don't get disappointed on your birthday when you open your presents. But you actually do care. Nothing else seems to matter if you don't get that one thing.

When your birthday rolls around, you sit among friends with cake and laughter. But inside, you're secretly hoping, "Is there any way I could have that one object I want so badly? Could it be possible that someone bought it for me?" As you unwrap gifts, you look around for a present that has a shape similar to that desirable possession. You don't see anything around that resembles it, but you still hope for the best. Present after present is opened. People have been kind and generous, and you decide to be very happy for what they have given you. But inside, you wish, "I wish there was more!" When all the gifts are opened, you thank everyone, but have trouble fighting off the feeling of disappointment.

But then it happens. Someone who loves you more than you

know says, "Oh yeah! There's one more gift!" They scurry off to another room to get it, and you think, "Could this be it? Is this the gift I was really wanting?" They come back in the room, and you carefully unwrap the present - half hopeful to see what you really wanted under the wrapping paper - and half scared that it won't be there.

And then you catch a glimpse. It's the gift! It's THE special, hoped-for, thought-about, longed-for item of your dreams. How could they afford such a lavish present? How were they able to get you such a thing? Is this for real?

You find out later that this person who loves you paid a huge price to get you what you wanted. They sold their car. They worked an extra job at night, and they ate very little for three months to be able to afford this for you. Wow. You are stunned. Even though you wanted the gift, it's even more valuable now, since you know what was done to purchase it. It is your most cherished possession. And you realize that you are loved - so much that this person sacrificed for you to receive the **best gift ever!**

I can think of a few things I'd like that cost much more than anyone could ever afford. Can you? But I don't expect anyone to sell their car, work extra hours, or go without food just to give me that gift. Who would do that for you or me?

Someone already has.

Up to this point, we have talked about the gifts God gave you in your **body** and **soul**…your personality, your spiritual gifts, your physical appearance. But we haven't discussed yet the most important part of you - **your spirit**. Your spirit is what will live forever. Long after your body is dead and buried, your spirit will be alive and spend eternity somewhere.

It's kind of hard to think about your spirit because we live every day so aware of how we **feel** and what we **look** like. But the spirit inside is you is the MOST IMPORTANT PART!

But there's a problem. Way back when Adam and Eve started the human race, there was this open relationship between them and God. Everything was perfect. The world had no sickness, no weeds and no tears. Adam and Eve walked and talked with God every day. But one choice changed it all.

They began to wonder if God really had their best interest in mind. After all, God made one rule - to not eat the fruit from ONE tree in the garden. Why would God do that? An enemy (who took on the form of a serpent) convinced them that God's plan wasn't the best for them. **As their trust in God slowly wore down, their hope to have something better on their own took over.** They took and ate forbidden fruit - the only thing God asked them not to do. The moment they ate it, something happened deep inside them. Their spirit died. Sin and death and darkness entered our world.And mankind was eternally separated from Love itself. The world has dealt with those problems ever since.

> *"When Adam sinned, sin entered the world.*
> *Adam's sin brought death, so death spread to everyone,*
> *for everyone sinned."*
> *(Romans 5:12 NLT)*

It may not look this way, but many of us are still walking around with 1/3 of us still dead inside. Sin has done it to us all. We laugh, we joke, we have fun. We attend school and college, get married, and raise families. We cry: we feel: we live our lives. But our spirit is not alive. It is not connected with God. The Bible describes it this way…

> *"At one time you were dead because of your sins."*
> *Ephesians 2:1 (NLV)*

We know we need something, but are not sure what. What we need is a spiritual fresh start. **We need a brand new heart.**

I hope you understand that I'm not talking about going to church or praying. Some of you are in a Christian environment already. I'm not talking about how you help others or sing worship songs on Sunday. As a matter of fact, I'm not talking about DOING good at all. **Doing good does not bring us any closer to God.**

The only way to have a new spirit is to receive the gift of Jesus Himself. Let me tell you a story…I was fortunate to grow up in a Christian home. I wanted desperately to serve Him and love Him my whole life. I was afraid of hell, and of course wanted to go to heaven! I sang in church, and eventually even worked on church staff. But the older I got, the more confused I became. I gave in every possible way - to others and to my church. I wanted to live completely for God and God alone. I sang about Him. I shared His Words with others. But I kept feeling afraid. Was I actually new inside myself?

Some people call it salvation. Jesus called it being born again. Whatever you call it, you know when you have it. And that was my problem. I wasn't sure. I prayed and begged God for help. And all I got was more confusion. Was *I* saved? Fear was my biggest motivator.

But one day it all changed. I sat in a wedding and a beautiful friend sang about Jesus and all He did for me. The song talked about the cross where He died. It talked about His blood, His pain, and His love. I had heard the story thousands of times. But I realized that I just had not received Him for myself.

I was so busy wanting to live for Him that He was standing back waiting to live IN me.

He was waiting for me to stop trying; waiting for me to let go; waiting for me to trust my life fully into His hands.

That day, during that song, I received Jesus. I received the fact that He paid for my sin. That He loved me enough to take me as I was. That He was good enough to walk with me my whole life long. That He was the faithful Friend I could count on. From that day on, I never questioned my salvation. I knew I had received Him and that was enough.

This became one of my favorite Bible verses:

"But as many as received Him, to them He gave the right to become children of God, to those who believe in His name."
John 1:12 (NKJV)

An amazing change takes place when we receive Jesus. The Bible says God looks at us as if we'd never sinned. He receives us as His child, and we begin a new journey of knowing and loving Him. You may not see or feel any different. **But your faith in God provided you the greatest gift of this lifetime - the gift of being transformed from the inside out.** The gift of being found "in Christ" instead of in your own sinful self.

Remember the movie *Beauty and the Beast*? The terrifying, ugly Beast longs to know and receive love from Beauty. But he is stuck in a body that is just…beastly. Nothing but magic could change him. And it does! It transforms his ugly, horrifying features into a handsome man…and they all live happily ever after …blah blah blah. Like that beast, we are unable to get ourselves out of the state we are in. On our best day, we are still not good enough to connect and know the amazing, perfect loving God of the universe. We need an intervention from some one greater than us. We need His power to make us new.

It's time to watch a video to remind you about what this looks like.

Small Group Leader, go to the "Small Group Leader" tab on our website and click on Chapter 5, Video Link #1.

When finished, watch Video Link #2 to finish this chapter. Remember to encourage the students to take notes!

VIDEO SESSION NOTES

"Anyone who belongs to Christ has become a _____ person. The old life is _____; a new life has begun!"
II Corinthians 5:17 (NLT)

What happens on the inside is this - your spirit becomes

_____

"For God so loved the world that He _____ His one and only Son that _____ who believes in Him shall not perish but have eternal life."
John 3:16 (NIV)

The gift God offers is a _____ _____
in exchange for every sin and flaw in you.

There's nothing you have to do for it. Only

_____.

"But as many as _____ Him, to them, He gave the _____ to become _____ of God, even to those who believe in His name"
John 1:12 (NASB)

Small Group Leader - Please ask the students to let you know if they received Christ today. If someone has, please email us TODAY at contactyouniquelydesigned@gmail.com

We want to share in this good news. Also, if comfortable, feel free to ask questions about the things discussed in today's lesson. What the students are wondering and asking is vital for us to be aware of and help answer. Thank you for partnering with us to help lead students into a relationship with Jesus.

CHECK ANY OF THE BOXES BELOW THAT APPLY TO YOU AND WRITE THE DATE ON THE BOTTOM OF THIS PAGE. THIS IS A REMARKABLE, AMAZING DAY FOR YOU!

☐ **Today, I received what Christ did for me and asked Him to lead my life from now on.**

☐ **Today, I gave my life to Jesus again. I've prayed for Him to take my life in the past, but I wanted to start fresh again today.**

☐ **I have more questions about salvation and what Jesus did for me.**

_____ / _____ / _____

CHAPTER 6

YOUR SUPERPOWER

Group Reading

I'm so glad you're back again! Can you believe we are already at Week #6? You've learned about your personality, found out what your major love language is, discovered the gifts given to you by your Creator, and have invited Him into your life to use you just as you are. WOW! These last 3 sessions are going to be the most exciting, so get ready…

For this session, we are going to do things a little differently. We will start with a fun movie clip and then watch a Video Session. We will end with our Group Reading. Let's get started!

Small Group Leader, go to the "Small Group Leader" tab on our website and click on Chapter 6, Video Link #1.

When finished, watch Video Link #2. Take the time to fill in the blanks in your book as you listen.

VIDEO SESSION NOTES

He promised to send a friend that _____,
_____, and _____ you. He
promised to give you His _____ _____

*"The Counselor, the Holy Spirit, whom the Father will send in my
name, will teach you all things and will remind you of
everything I said to you."*
John 14:26 (WEB)

Maybe you have no idea what the _____ inside
YOU can do, and the incredible _____ it
will have on the world around you!

If God is in you, then you have access to _____
powerful because of Him.

*"...the Spirit of him who raised Jesus from the dead
is living in you..."*
Rom. 8:11a (NIV)

You have a _____ to get to know the Holy
Spirit and see His power in your life.

God actually specializes in taking things that are
_____ or in _____, and turning the
person or situation around to be _____.

*"And we have this treasure in earthen vessels, that the excellency of
the power may be of God, and not of us".*
II Cor 4:7 (YLT)

THERE ARE PARTS OF MY LIFE WHERE I REALLY
NEED GOD'S POWER. THEY ARE...

_____

_____

_____

_____

_____

_____

Group Reading

I have a driving story to tell you, but before I do, I need you to promise that you will NEVER try this. I can't believe I ever did such a stupid thing, and I am very lucky to live to tell about it. Here goes. I was a young twenty-something and a girlfriend and I were driving in a caravan of cars down to Florida. She had been at the wheel a long time, and was getting tired. Because we didn't want to make everyone else stop, we decided that we could probably switch seats - if we were very careful - WHILE THE CAR WAS GOING 70 MILES AN HOUR DOWN THE ROAD. Thanks to the cruise control button, we didn't have to press the accelerator. The car would drive a consistent 70 mph until a foot hit the brake.

The trick was sliding from the passenger seat to the driver's seat, and grabbing the wheel at just the right time when my friend let go. She shimmied her way over the gear shift and headed for my lap. I slid underneath her as she continued to extend her arm far enough to steer the car. Finally, I squeezed into the driver's seat as she let go of the wheel. The car gave a little jerk in the lane, and we may have had a few cars beep at us as we sped by. Whew! We lived to tell the tale.

Besides the obvious lesson to never put your life in such danger, this story may help you visualize a simple truth. You can't have two people in the driver's seat driving at the same time. **One has to let go in order for the other person to do the driving.**

That is what walking with God is like. This is a key to receiving God's power. You can take control of the steering wheel of your life any time you want. But you and He cannot drive at the same time. **Either He is in control or you are in charge.** This requires faith as you keep trusting your life into His hands. This requires regular communication with God. This is what a relationship with God is all about!

Have you ever known someone who called themselves a Christian, and their actions made you think, "If that's what a Christian is, I don't want to be one!" I've met those kind of people, too, and I'm sorry if you've had that experience. The truth is Christians aren't automatically loving, God-filled, compassionate, cool people to be with. They have to follow Jesus to be that way!

You have the option to grow and become more like Jesus. Or you have the option to stay the same.

CHECK OUT THIS SCRIPTURE...

"For you are still only baby Christians, controlled by your own desires, not God's. ... doesn't that prove you are still babies, wanting your own way? In fact, you are acting like people who don't belong to the Lord at all."
1 Corinthians 3:3 (TLB)

So, what are you controlled by? Are you mostly controlled by your own desires? Do you usually need things to be your way? If I'm honest, I find that I often am living the way I want to. How about you? In the meter below, shade in an honest assessment of yourself.

I AM IN CONTROL
& WANT THINGS
TO GO MY WAY

GOD IS IN CONTROL
OF MY LIFE
ALWAYS

There are some clear verses in the Bible that help us know if we are guided by the Holy Spirit or not. I use this as a checkpoint to see what category my heart is being controlled by...

"I say this to you: Let the Holy Spirit lead you in each step. Then you will not please your sinful old selves. The things our old selves want to do are against what the Holy Spirit wants. The Holy Spirit does not agree with what our sinful old selves want. These two are against each other...

__The things your sinful old self wants to do are:__ sex sins (sex outside of marriage), sinful desires, wild living, worshiping false gods, witchcraft, hating, fighting, being jealous, being angry, arguing, dividing into little groups and thinking the other groups are wrong, false teaching, wanting something someone else has, killing other people, using strong drink (getting drunk), wild parties, and all things like these. I told you before and I am telling you again that those who do these things will have no place in the holy nation of God.

__But the fruit that comes from having the Holy Spirit in our lives is:__ love, joy, peace, not giving up, being kind, being good, having faith, being gentle, and being the boss over our own desires…If the Holy Spirit is living in us, let us be led by Him in all things."
Galatians 5:16-17, 19-23, 25 (NLV)

When we read a list like that, we can get discouraged. How can I possibly live like that? **The key is not to try harder.** If you use all your own effort to change, you will only get frustrated. **The key is surrender.** The key is that God wants to fill you and help you. The key is His super-power - the Holy Spirit.

"Apart from faith in Christ, you cannot become a Christian, and apart from moment by moment faith or dependence on Him, you cannot live the Christian life. When you are filled with the Holy Spirit, Christ lives His supernatural life in and through you."
~Bill Bright

Let's do a little recap. When you receive Christ, He comes on the inside forever in all His power. **But how much you allow God to live through you is up to you**. There is a difference between being a Christian and being full of God.

Because we are human, we need something that continually helps us past our natural way of living. We need to be filled with the Holy Spirit. God knows we need His help so much that He actually commands us to be filled with Him!

"Do not get drunk with wine. That leads to wild living. Instead, be filled with the Holy Spirit."
Ephesians 5:18 (NLV)

Those words "be filled" mean "be continually filled" or "keep on being filled." Not only is it a command, it's something that can happen over and over again. It's a benefit we have all day every day.

Here are 4 steps that can help you in the future. When you find you need the Holy Spirit and His power...

1. STOP

2. CONFESS

3. ASK

4. RECEIVE

1. STOP:

Take a quick pause and stop what you are doing. Reflect for a moment. "What's going on in my heart? What's going on around me? **Am I in control or is God?"**

2. CONFESS

You can't be filled up with God and filled with sin or selfish desires at the same time. If you find that you are anxious, worried, overwhelmed, angry, upset, depressed, jealous, or anything else sinful, confess it to God. Tell Him that you recognize these things in your heart and honestly confess them as a sin. **Talk to Him like a friend.** He wants to help you. He doesn't need you to fix yourself first before you come to Him. Come just as you are and present it all with honesty. He will always forgive you and cleanse your heart from the effects of sin.

3. ASK

God promises that if we ask, He will fill us. **We ask. He fills.**

"If you then…know how to give good gifts to your children, how much more will your Father in heaven give the Holy Spirit to those who ask him!"
Luke 11:13 (NIV)

Say something to Him like, "God, thank you that you promised to give the Holy Spirit to anyone who asks. I ask you to fill me now with your Holy Spirit."

4. RECEIVE

The same way you received salvation and forgiveness (by faith) is the same way you receive the filling of the Holy Spirit. It's not about a feeling - although sometimes you may feel Him. It's not about a cool experience, although you may have some very cool experiences with Him. **It's about believing that God will answer you because He promises He will.**

"This is the confidence we have in approaching God: that if we ask anything according to his will, He hears us."
I John 5:14 (NIV)

It's His will for you to be filled. And He is hearing you. Have confidence that He will fill you because you asked. What happens when you are filled? First of all, you have a happier, more loving, peace-filled nature that you don't naturally have on your own. Your heart is filled with more love, and sometimes even a song. He begins to put His desires in you. He works in you His will. You will want to spend more time with Him, and you will want to read His Word. It becomes easier to trust Him and obey what He asks of you. You will have more love for others. You will want to share your love for Christ with others. You find peace easier in stressful situations...and so much more!

The filled life = the best life!

Let's end this section by going through our four steps and asking God to fill us. Remember?

The steps are STOP, CONFESS, ASK, RECEIVE.

Small Group Leaders, please take over and lead them in this prayer. Using the chart from a few pages ago, let the students confess to God their specific need for Him and where they recognize they fall short. Then ask Him in faith to fill you, and see what God does!

CHAPTER 7

THE WHISPER THAT CHANGES EVERYTHING

Group Reading

Hey! I hope you had a great week and are ready to grow some more today. Last week we talked about accessing God's power. It will take just one time experiencing God working through you, and you'll be hooked! Was there a time you remembered to STOP, CONFESS, ASK and RECEIVE?

Take few minutes to chat about that in your group, then continue.

When I was growing up, we did not have the internet. The cool kids had video games, but many of us either couldn't afford them or were not allowed to play with them regularly. That left us staring at each other, or coming up with fun things to do.

One of the activities my brother and I tried was making our own "phones" that allowed us to talk to each other from long distances. It worked like this. You take two cups and put a small hole in the bottom of each. Then you thread a string through each hole and tie a knot at each end. Last, each person would take a cup in opposite directions and pull the string tight. Sitting in separate rooms, we could talk to each other and hear one another clearly using the cups as a receiver - as long as the string was tight. That was the secret. If the string went limp, our voices could no longer carry. It was a fun game. We could pretend we were spies doing secret agent activity or some other crazy adventure. Ok, maybe it was a little lame, but for us, it was cool.

Imagine you and God each holding that cup. He is on one end and you are on the other. He could be talking to you all day long, but if that string isn't tight to carry His voice to your ears, you won't hear Him! It would be frustrating because you would know He was right there speaking, but you couldn't tell what He was saying. **Maybe the trouble we have hearing God's voice is because the line between us isn't right.** Maybe it's the connection that's missing. Maybe God is speaking more than you know, but you haven't recognized it as Him, or the connection between you needs to be different. Let's think about that for a minute.

Take a moment to circle yes or no to the following questions…

Do you have trouble seeing God in your every day world?

YES   NO

Does God seem like someone you know about, but you don't know how to make Him a part of your every day with school, home, friendships, etc?

YES   NO

Do you daily ask Him questions and involve Him in your choices?

YES   NO

Do you recognize when He's leading or speaking to you?

YES   NO

The great news is that whether you marked yes or no to the previous answers, those answers can change.

You can get as close to God as you want Him to be.

"Come close to God, and God will come close to you."
James 4:8a (NLT)

This is a promise God made that we can count on. When you feel far from God, take a step towards Him, and He will always come close to you. How do we actually do that? How do we go from God feeling far away, to walking and talking with Him? **We have to strengthen our connection.**

But let's settle first that God is speaking.

CHECK OUT THIS SCRIPTURE...

"Wisdom shouts in the streets. She cries out in the public square. She calls to the crowds along the main street, to those gathered in front of the city gate: 'How long, you simpletons, will you insist on being simpleminded?... Come and listen to my counsel. I'll share my heart with you and make you wise.'"
Proverbs 1: 20-23 (NLT)

God's wisdom is available everywhere. Some of it is meant to be searched out...like scientists who discover the cure to a disease. Some of it is obvious....like you should stop at a stop sign or you might get hit by a car. Some of His wisdom is personal - YOUnique whispers meant for you to hear for YOUR personal life. I want to help you recognize and hear His voice with more clarity. **I want you to have the confidence that comes when you KNOW He has spoken.**

So, what does God's voice sound like? Let's look for some examples in the Bible.

Elijah was one of the most incredible, godly men who ever lived. His story is found in the Bible. As a prophet, he spoke to others for God, and performed amazing miracles. After calling fire down from heaven to show God's power to His people (wow), he became afraid of an evil queen who threatened to kill him. He ran far away, and was desperate for an answer. This is how the Bible describes God speaking to him.

*The Lord said, "Go out and stand on the mountain in the presence of the Lord, for the Lord is about to pass by." Then a great and powerful wind tore the mountains apart and shattered the rocks before the Lord, but the Lord was not in the wind. After the wind there was an earthquake, but the Lord was not in the earthquake. After the earthquake came a fire, but the Lord was not in the fire. And after the fire came **a gentle whisper.***
I Kings 19:11-12 (NIV)

We can often describe God's voice as a whisper...an impression on your heart or mind. Have you ever heard a little voice tell you that it would be smart to do something, and later on realized that you should have listened to it?

That little voice is the voice of wisdom.

That little voice is God's way of speaking to us.

That little voice will save your life.

Make it a priority to hear and recognize that voice!

It's time for our video sessions! First, you will watch a video clip of sheep in a field being called by several strangers. Only when the shepherd calls, do they come.

Small Group Leader, go to the "Small Group Leader" tab on our website and click on Chapter 7, Video Link #1.

When finished, watch Video Link #2. Remember to encourage students to take notes.

VIDEO SESSION NOTES

"The sheep _____ His voice and _____
to him. He _____ his own sheep by name and
_____ them out. He _____ ahead of
them, and they follow him because they know his_____.
They won't follow a stranger; they will run from him because they
don't know his_____."
John 10:2b-5 (NLT)

It may take time, but God's _____
will be able to recognize if He's _____
to them.

How to hear God's voice more clearly...

1. You have to _____ to hear it.

Maybe God is waiting to see what you do with
something He's already spoken to you before He
gives you more.

God uses _____ to help guide us.
Ramp up how you listen to _____,
and you may find you start hearing _____.

2. You have to be in the right _____

_____.

If your life is filled with too much busy activity
(even good things), you won't have any space or

time to stop and hear the whispers God is speaking to you.

1. Set aside _____ to read the Bible.

2. Make space for _____.

3. Find a _____ of people who love God, you can hang out with regularly, and "do life" with.

Group Reading

It takes a little practice to recognize God's voice. But once you feel you have heard Him (no matter how important or unimportant it may be) there are a couple ways you can test to see if what you heard is from the LORD.

HOW DO I KNOW I HEARD FROM GOD?

1. Ask yourself: **Am I genuinely wanting God's will in my life or am I wanting my own way in an area?** Check your heart first for its motive. If your heart is clear, then move on! If you are holding on to anxiety, worry, or YOUR opinion and desire, go back to our 4 step plan…STOP, CONFESS, ASK, RECEIVE.

2. **Does it come from a heart of love?** God IS love (I John 4:8) so everything He speaks comes from love, even correction.

3. **Does it agree with what the Bible says?** The Bible has so much to say about our personal lives - from finances to relationships. His Word is truth, so He will NEVER contradict what is found in His Word.

4. **What do other godly people in my life say?** The input of others who love God is a great way to protect yourself from going in a direction that is unwise. Ask close friends and spiritual authority what they think about what you heard.

After you have gone through the four-step test, step out and DO something with what you heard Him say. Take an action step. The cool thing about God is that, even if you are wrong, He will help correct your direction as you go. He simply says,

> *"Test everything that is said. Hold on to what is good."*
> *I Thess 5:21 (NLT)*

I love that! Basically, He's saying, "If it's from me, it's going to be good, and it will come to pass!" The most obvious way to know God is speaking is that you will see His Words to you fulfilled.

He never lies.

Have you heard the Lord speaking to you? Even in this lesson, there were probably a few things that stuck out to you. That is HIM! I call it the "holy high-lighter"…when I read or hear something that seems to jump up at me from the page. The whisper of the Holy Spirit is touching your heart when that happens.

Take a few minutes for your group to silently reflect on what was shared today. Look at the following questions and write down your answers in the book.

Small Group Leader, please facilitate a time for quiet reflection. You are welcome to play quiet worship music as the students write in their books.

This stuck out to me in the lesson today:

_____

_____

_____

Identify a time when you felt close to God in the past. What feeling did His presence bring? What did He say to you or impress on your heart at that moment?

_____

_____

_____

Now, ask God if He has anything else He wants to say to you. Literally, ask Him to speak to you. Listen quietly, and if you hear something, write it down.

_____

_____

_____

List an action step you can take this week based on something you felt God say to you above.

_____

_____

_____

Small Group Leader, when everyone looks finished, ask the students if anyone wants to share what they wrote down. There is no pressure, but it is encouraging to hear what others hear from the Lord!

Group Reading

As you finish this chapter, be encouraged. Some of you may easily hear and recognize God's voice. Others may still be wondering if you EVER heard from Him. That's okay. This is a relationship journey. And we all have a YOUnique path to walk with Him. But you can take that first step by asking Him to speak to you.

If you are an introvert, you may feel closer to God when you are alone…whether outside, reading a book, listening to music, or resting. For the extrovert, you may feel more connected with God in a crowd of people - at church, talking with friends, or in a worship environment. God has YOUniquely infinite ways to speak to us. Just keep putting yourself in the right environments and keep reading the Bible. No matter how He chooses to speak to you, rest assured. **He YOUniquely wants to walk and talk with you every day.**

CHECK OUT THIS SCRIPTURE...

"Your ears will hear a word behind you, 'This is the way, walk in it,' whenever you turn to the right or to the left."

Isaiah 30:21 (NIV)

CHAPTER 8

BIG DREAMS & BIG GOALS

Group Reading

Do you ever think to yourself, "What do I want to do with my life?" or "Who do I want to be?" Have you ever thought, "I wonder what I'm really going to be like 10 or 20 years from now?"

You may not realize it, but every step you take today is bringing you closer to a goal - even if you don't know what the goal is. That's because:

EVERY DAY COUNTS.

It may seem like just another ordinary day with school work or chores. It may feel like things are awfully boring in your world. You may find yourself busy looking at other people's lives on social media and wish for some of that for yourself, as you sit at home and do nothing.

But all you have is today. And you. And God. **And every minute we breathe, we are making choices.** And all those choices build up over time to create the big things you hope for and want in your life.

The kind of attitude you have, the way you treat your friends, the respect you give adults, what you do when no one is looking, how you spend your free time, how you take care of yourself, how you eat, what you watch on TV….all these things are small little choices that over time make a big impact. Imagine that you are to walk in a straight line from point A to point B. If you are just a few degrees off, eventually you will be miles away from point B and in a completely different place - point C!

And the longer you go that way, the further off you will be from your goal. Instead of leaving things to chance, you can take **small steps every day that lead you in** time to an incredible place you never dreamed possible. One thing is for sure,

"With God, ALL things are possible!"
Matthew 19:26 (NIV)

So, God wants us to know that our lives aren't just random occurrences with no meaning or value. There is purpose for it all and our **choices** take us either in a good or bad direction.

"For we are God's handiwork, created in Christ Jesus to do good works, which God prepared in advance for us to do."
Ephesians 2:10 (NIV)

Wow! What could those good works be? It may be something you do that helps somebody else, but no one ever knows except you and God. It may be something you do for yourself that you know is the right thing to do. It may be something that thousands of people see and applaud. Either way, it all matters to

God. Remember, God wants to use every person for His special purpose - and He's looking around the earth to find people who want to say yes to Him. (II Chronicles 16:9)

That makes me want to say, "Pick me! Pick me!"

So...I ask you...where are you heading? Where would you like to be in the future? What are you dreaming about?

All that gifting in you is for a purpose. God combines those gifts in you with the dreams you have for your future and sets you on a direction towards "HIMpossible," exciting, and adventurous living.

So let me ask you again...what are you dreaming? Has this ever crossed your mind: "I want to do this..."

Well, it's time to write it down. Today, you're going to create a Bucket List. It's a fun list of all the things you would like to do before you kick the bucket (a nice description for dying). Have fun and think of impossible things. Think of practical things. Think of things you'd like to do, or have seen someone else do and you want to try. Consider topics like adventure, career, family, accomplishments, relationships, vacations...
You have 5-10 minutes to write. You probably will want to add to the list over time, but this is a great way to start. Now, go for it, and have fun dreaming!

MY BUCKET LIST:
BEFORE I DIE, I WANT TO...

_____

_____

_____

_____

_____

_____

_____

_____

_____

Small Group Leader, please give about 10 minutes for the students to complete their lists. Encourage them to write at least 5-10 things down, and hopefully more! When time is up, gather together and let a few willing students share some of the things they wrote on their list.

When finished, go to the "Small Group Leader" tab on our website and click on Chapter 8, Video Link #1.

VIDEO SESSION NOTES

If you want all the things on your Bucket List to come to pass, the best way is to work from the

_____ _____.

_____ and the _____ things in life always come from what's _____ you, not what is on the outside.

Discuss the following questions in your group. Choose a few famous people that you all know - movie stars, famous sports players, or political leaders. Using those specific people's names, discuss the answers to these questions:

1. What are they known for? (What did they accomplish?)
2. Is there anything they could do that would change how people think about them?
3. Does fame and achieving big goals mean that a person has been successful in their life?
4. Which is more important…What you accomplish or who you become as a person? Why?
5. What's better? Your character or what you do?

After answering these questions as a group, turn on the video again.

_____ you _____ on the inside is more important than _____ you _____ on the outside.

What God is doing _____ you is more important than anything _____ could _____ for Him.

Happiness will come from God's presence (the _____) rather than His presents (the _____).

Look at the list of words below and circle the top 5 things most important to you. In your lifetime, what do you want to be remembered for?

Prosperity	Leadership	Truthfulness
Patience	Diligence	Social Media
Love	Popularity	Fame
Beauty	Wealth	Knowledge
Friendship	Sports Talent	Career
Being Smart	Achievement	Trustworthiness
Kindness	Family	Relationships
Making a Difference in People's Lives	Happiness	Peace
	Hard Work	Wisdom
Fun	Thankfulness	Health
Contentment	Generosity	Self-Control
Great Looks	Most Likes on Social Media	Big House
Knowing/Loving God		

VALUES THAT ARE IMPORTANT TO ME THAT ARE AMORAL.
I CAN'T SEE MY LIFE WITHOUT...

_____

_____

_____

_____

_____

_____

It's time to be _____ about the direction I'm heading.

"A GOAL IS A DREAM WITH A DEADLINE."
—NAPOLEON HILL

Small Group Leader, at the end of Video Session #1, give the students some time to complete their Goal Chart for the year. If you are meeting in the first half of the year, fill out the FIRST goal chart. If you are meeting in the second half of the year, fill out the SECOND chart (1/2 Year Update). Encourage the students to revisit these goal lists every 6 months until they graduate. There are enough charts in the book to start in 6th grade and continue through 12th grade. Remember - the important thing is to DO it, not make it perfect. It can always be changed. Also, encourage students to share their goals with their parents. Before leaving this meeting, have the students share one thing that they wrote down as a goal for themselves.

Group Reading:
Congratulations! You've completed the YOUnique experience. It's been an amazing 8 weeks with you. Long before you ever picked up this book, I was praying for you. Each of your lives are so important. I would love to hear how YOUnique has helped you personally because your lives are the fire that keep me going. Please take a minute to watch a personal video from me as you prepare to leave. Also, be sure to share your stories on social media. That way, I can see your faces and enjoy your YOUnique experience with you. Use the hashag:

#YOUniquely_Designed

I'm praying for you all and am believing that God will do GREAT things through YOU!

Small Group Leader, go to the "Small Group Leader" tab on our website and click on Video Link #2 to conclude the YOUnique experience!

My Goals for the Year:

$$\boxed{}$$

The Character Trait I want to Focus on is:

$$\boxed{}$$

Spiritual - What one thing can I do to get closer to God?_____

_____

_____

_____

Physical - How can I help my body be healthy? _____

_____

_____

_____

Is there anything I want to accomplish this year physically? (specific sports, races, etc.) _____

_____

_____

_____

Educational - What do I want to accomplish in school this year?

_____

_____

_____

Talent - What talent can I develop this year and how? (ideas: sports, music abilities, writing, baking, sewing, carpentry, acting, film-making...the list is endless)

_____

_____

_____

Family - What area can I grow in in this year to be a better brother/sister and daughter/son? _____

_____

_____

What spiritual gift can I use to help others and how?

_____

_____

_____

A Bible verse about the Character trait I chose is (google it if you don't know one): _____

_____

_____

Other: _____

_____

_____

_____

My 1/2 Year Update:

The Character Trait I want to Focus on is:

Spiritual - What one thing can I do to get closer to God?_____

_____

_____

_____

Physical - How can I help my body be healthy? _____

_____

_____

Is there anything I want to accomplish this year physically? (specific sports, races, etc.) _____

_____

_____

Educational - What do I want to accomplish in school this year?

_____

_____

_____

Talent - What talent can I develop this year and how? (ideas: sports, music abilities, writing, baking, sewing, carpentry, acting, film-making…the list is endless)

_____

_____

_____

Family - What area can I grow in in this year to be a better brother/sister and daughter/son? _____

_____

_____

What spiritual gift can I use to help others and how?

_____

_____

_____

A Bible verse about the Character trait I chose is (google it if you don't know one): _____

_____ _____

_____

Other: _____

_____

_____

My Goals for the Year:

[ ]

The Character Trait I want to Focus on is:

[ ]

Spiritual - What one thing can I do to get closer to God?_____
_____
_____
_____

Physical - How can I help my body be healthy? _____
_____
_____
_____

Is there anything I want to accomplish this year physically? (specific sports, races, etc.) _____
_____
_____
_____

Educational - What do I want to accomplish in school this year?
_____
_____
_____

Talent - What talent can I develop this year and how? (ideas: sports, music abilities, writing, baking, sewing, carpentry, acting, film-making…the list is endless)

_____

_____

_____

Family - What area can I grow in in this year to be a better brother/sister and daughter/son? _____

_____

_____

What spiritual gift can I use to help others and how?

_____

_____

_____

A Bible verse about the Character trait I chose is (google it if you don't know one): _____

_____

_____

Other: _____

_____

_____

_____

My 1/2 Year Update:

The Character Trait I want to Focus on is:

Spiritual - What one thing can I do to get closer to God?_____

_____

_____

_____

Physical - How can I help my body be healthy? _____

_____

_____

Is there anything I want to accomplish this year physically? (specific sports, races, etc.) _____

_____

_____

Educational - What do I want to accomplish in school this year?

_____

_____

_____

Talent - What talent can I develop this year and how? (ideas: sports, music abilities, writing, baking, sewing, carpentry, acting, film-making…the list is endless)

_____

_____

_____

Family - What area can I grow in in this year to be a better brother/sister and daughter/son? _____

_____

_____

What spiritual gift can I use to help others and how?

_____

_____

_____

A Bible verse about the Character trait I chose is (google it if you don't know one): _____

_____   _____

_____

Other: _____

_____

_____

My Goals for the Year:

The Character Trait I want to Focus on is:

Spiritual - What one thing can I do to get closer to God?_____
_____
_____
_____

Physical - How can I help my body be healthy? _____
_____
_____
_____

Is there anything I want to accomplish this year physically? (specific sports, races, etc.) _____
_____
_____
_____

Educational - What do I want to accomplish in school this year?
_____
_____
_____

Talent - What talent can I develop this year and how? (ideas: sports, music abilities, writing, baking, sewing, carpentry, acting, film-making…the list is endless)

_____

_____

_____

Family - What area can I grow in in this year to be a better brother/sister and daughter/son? _____

_____

_____

What spiritual gift can I use to help others and how?

_____

_____

_____

A Bible verse about the Character trait I chose is (google it if you don't know one): _____

_____

_____

Other: _____

_____

_____

_____

My 1/2 Year Update:

[ ]

The Character Trait I want to Focus on is:

[ ]

Spiritual - What one thing can I do to get closer to God?_____
_____
_____
_____

Physical - How can I help my body be healthy? _____
_____
_____

Is there anything I want to accomplish this year physically? (specific sports, races, etc.) _____
_____
_____

Educational - What do I want to accomplish in school this year?
_____
_____
_____

Talent - What talent can I develop this year and how? (ideas: sports, music abilities, writing, baking, sewing, carpentry, acting, film-making…the list is endless)

_____

_____

_____

Family - What area can I grow in in this year to be a better brother/sister and daughter/son? _____

_____

_____

What spiritual gift can I use to help others and how?

_____

_____

_____

A Bible verse about the Character trait I chose is (google it if you don't know one): _____

_____ _____

_____

Other: _____

_____

_____

My Goals for the Year:

The Character Trait I want to Focus on is:

Spiritual - What one thing can I do to get closer to God?_____

_____

_____

_____

Physical - How can I help my body be healthy? _____

_____

_____

_____

Is there anything I want to accomplish this year physically? (specific sports, races, etc.) _____

_____

_____

_____

Educational - What do I want to accomplish in school this year?

_____

_____

_____

Talent - What talent can I develop this year and how? (ideas: sports, music abilities, writing, baking, sewing, carpentry, acting, film-making…the list is endless)

_____

_____

_____

Family - What area can I grow in in this year to be a better brother/sister and daughter/son? _____

_____

_____

What spiritual gift can I use to help others and how?

_____

_____

_____

A Bible verse about the Character trait I chose is (google it if you don't know one): _____

_____

_____

Other: _____

_____

_____

_____

My 1/2 Year Update:

> [   ]

The Character Trait I want to Focus on is:

> [   ]

Spiritual - What one thing can I do to get closer to God?_____

_____

_____

_____

Physical - How can I help my body be healthy? _____

_____

_____

Is there anything I want to accomplish this year physically? (specific sports, races, etc.) _____

_____

_____

Educational - What do I want to accomplish in school this year?

_____

_____

_____

Talent - What talent can I develop this year and how? (ideas: sports, music abilities, writing, baking, sewing, carpentry, acting, film-making…the list is endless)

_____

_____

_____

Family - What area can I grow in in this year to be a better brother/sister and daughter/son? _____

_____

_____

What spiritual gift can I use to help others and how?

_____

_____

_____

A Bible verse about the Character trait I chose is (google it if you don't know one): _____

_____ _____

_____

Other: _____

_____

_____

My Goals for the Year:

The Character Trait I want to Focus on is:

Spiritual - What one thing can I do to get closer to God?_____

_____

_____

_____

Physical - How can I help my body be healthy? _____

_____

_____

_____

Is there anything I want to accomplish this year physically? (specific sports, races, etc.) _____

_____

_____

_____

Educational - What do I want to accomplish in school this year?

_____

_____

_____

Talent - What talent can I develop this year and how? (ideas: sports, music abilities, writing, baking, sewing, carpentry, acting, film-making...the list is endless)

_____

_____

_____

Family - What area can I grow in in this year to be a better brother/sister and daughter/son? _____

_____

_____

What spiritual gift can I use to help others and how?

_____

_____

_____

A Bible verse about the Character trait I chose is (google it if you don't know one): _____

_____

_____

Other: _____

_____

_____

_____

My 1/2 Year Update:

> [   ]

The Character Trait I want to Focus on is:

> [   ]

Spiritual - What one thing can I do to get closer to God?_____

_____

_____

_____

Physical - How can I help my body be healthy? _____

_____

_____

Is there anything I want to accomplish this year physically? (specific sports, races, etc.) _____

_____

_____

Educational - What do I want to accomplish in school this year?

_____

_____

_____

Talent - What talent can I develop this year and how? (ideas: sports, music abilities, writing, baking, sewing, carpentry, acting, film-making...the list is endless)

_____

_____

_____

Family - What area can I grow in in this year to be a better brother/sister and daughter/son? _____

_____

_____

What spiritual gift can I use to help others and how?

_____

_____

_____

A Bible verse about the Character trait I chose is (google it if you don't know one): _____

_____ _____

_____

Other: _____

_____

_____

My Goals for the Year:

The Character Trait I want to Focus on is:

Spiritual - What one thing can I do to get closer to God?_____

_____

_____

_____

Physical - How can I help my body be healthy? _____

_____

_____

_____

Is there anything I want to accomplish this year physically? (specific sports, races, etc.) _____

_____

_____

_____

Educational - What do I want to accomplish in school this year?

_____

_____

_____

Talent - What talent can I develop this year and how? (ideas: sports, music abilities, writing, baking, sewing, carpentry, acting, film-making...the list is endless)

_____

_____

_____

Family - What area can I grow in in this year to be a better brother/sister and daughter/son? _____

_____

_____

What spiritual gift can I use to help others and how?

_____

_____

_____

A Bible verse about the Character trait I chose is (google it if you don't know one): _____

_____

_____

Other: _____

_____

_____

_____

My 1/2 Year Update:

The Character Trait I want to Focus on is:

Spiritual - What one thing can I do to get closer to God?_____
_____
_____
_____

Physical - How can I help my body be healthy? _____
_____
_____

Is there anything I want to accomplish this year physically? (specific sports, races, etc.) _____
_____
_____

Educational - What do I want to accomplish in school this year?
_____
_____
_____

Talent - What talent can I develop this year and how? (ideas: sports, music abilities, writing, baking, sewing, carpentry, acting, film-making…the list is endless)

_____

_____

_____

Family - What area can I grow in in this year to be a better brother/sister and daughter/son? _____

_____

_____

What spiritual gift can I use to help others and how?

_____

_____

_____

A Bible verse about the Character trait I chose is (google it if you don't know one): _____

_____ _____

_____

Other: _____

_____

_____

ACKNOWLEDGEMENTS

No project like this is accomplished without the help of many people. Special thanks to…

Doug, my husband and life-long Love, for constant encouragement to keep going, insight, wisdom, and for managing the house and kids so I could have pockets of time away to do what was in my heart to do.

My "Fearless Threesome" friends - Jeannie, Lizzy & Erin for prayer support and encouragement to seek after God's call regardless of our present circumstances. You were part of this project in heart and soul.

Jennifer & Alissa for taking words and making them beautiful and alive on these pages.

Jordyn for designing a web-site that clearly carries the YOUnique message to the world.

Charlton and Erica for bringing your heart and soul to the video teaching series, and Trip for making the videos come to life

Valerie and Dennis for believing in something before you ever saw it, and generously giving to launch this experience.

For Ashley who gave up space in her house to provide a safe-haven to write.

For every parent and teen I spoke with whose need and stories ignited the fire for YOUnique to be born.

For Church of the Highlands, my home, where Spirit-led living is seen every day, and God's extraordinary grace and favor is tangible in the people and ministries that abound.

NOTES

The students are led to a great resource in chapter one in order to identify their personality type. This web-site provides the Myers Briggs personality test for teenagers. I'm grateful for such a specific resource. The online address is: http://www.interactiontalks.com/myers-briggs-personality-types-of-teenagers/

In C hapter Two, we discuss the "5 Love Languages." This is a concept that Dr. Gary Chapman discovered and wrote about in his book, *The Five Love Languages: The Secret to Love that Lasts*. The information we share with the students is based off of his teaching. We also use his online "Love Language Profiler for Teens" found at: http://www.5lovelanguages.com/profile/teens/

The teaching of spiritual gifts was gathered from many resources, most importantly the Bible. However, when the gifts are articulated in detail, we used one resource for consistency purposes. Jeff Carver provided a great teaching tool & online spiritual gifts test for youth. We use that online resource for students to discover their gifts. It can be found at: http://www.spiritualgiftstest.com/test/youth

Nick Fujicic's story is found online at: https://youtu.be/GSayMXTaQY8

Trousdale, G., Wise, K., Hahn, D., Woolverton, L., O'Hara, P., Benson, R., White, R., ... Walt Disney Studios Home Entertainment (Firm). (2010). *Beauty and the Beast*. Burbank, CA: Walt Disney Studios Home Entertainment.

Bird, B., Walker, J., Lasseter, J., Lucroy, J., Lin, P., Jimenez, A., Nelson, C.T., Buena Vista Home Entertainment (Firm) (2005). *The Incredibles*. Burbank, CA: Walt Disney Studios Home Entertainment

49100924R00064

Made in the USA
San Bernardino, CA
20 August 2019